THE SWALE AND RIVER MEDWAY ESTUARY   [923723] [20-6-72]

Looking over Queenborough to the mouth of the Swale and the River Medway Estuary. Chetney Marshes occupy the centre of the picture with Stangate Creek beyond. The ships on the far bank of the Medway are docked at the former oil refinery on the Isle of Grain, now dismantled. The distinctive outline of a sailing barge can be made out in the mouth of the Swale.

QUEENBOROUGH [909723] [7-7-71]

This view shows Queenborough in more detail with its once busy creek dividing the lower-left quadrant and the impressive High Street immediately above. To the right of the picture, just below centre, is the former school, its playground lying over part of the castle site, defined as the large circular earthwork between the school and the railway station.

SHEERNESS [908751] [26-5-61]

The former Royal Naval Dockyard at Sheerness has since closed down, but is now a thriving commercial port. The area right-of-centre is Blue Town. The seafront and fun fair can just be made out at the extreme right edge.

SHEERNESS [910733] [13-6-67]

Panorama looking north-east towards the seafront. The wide dark line running through the centre of the photograph is the defensive moat, known as the Barton's Point and Queenborough Lines, built to protect the landward approaches of Sheerness Dockyard. Today it is partly used as a boating lake.

MINSTER, SHEPPEY   [956730] [13-6-67]

The abbey church of SS. Mary and Sexburga sits prominently on a hill near the centre of the photograph, clearly visible for miles around. Although much of Minster has been developed as a very pleasant seaside town, at its heart is a very ancient settlement of old houses.

LEYSDOWN AND WARDEN   [012735] [13-6-67]

Panorama looking south-east over the crumbling cliffs at Warden Point to Leysdown, with Shellness beyond. The outline of the Swale is clearly defined here with Seasalter on the opposite bank, on the mainland, to the left of the picture.

SITTINGBOURNE [890650] [14-6-62]

Looking south-east along the A2 before the growth of the Eurolink Industrial Estate. The railway station can be seen just left-of-centre, with the branch line to Sheerness in the bottom-left corner. Bapchild is situated just above the centre with Teynham at the point where the A2 kinks to the right. (Compare with the similar view on back cover taken three years later.)

FAVERSHAM [015614] [3-6-56]

*An early view of the town taken before pedestrianisation and its designation as a conservation town. The Guildhall is clearly visible just left-of-centre, with the parish church situated top-centre.

GRAVENEY [053631] [4-1-78]

This fascinating vertical view of Graveney and Luddenham Marshes shows an aspect of Kent not often realised: the ancient division of land into a patchwork of small, irregularly shaped fields, here made more attractive by the numerous water channels and drainage ditches. Graveney church is situated about one-third of the way up the picture, in the centre.

DUNKIRK   [069589] [26-6-75]

Panorama looking east-south-east, showing the A2 bypass under construction. The parish church is situated just below centre. Canterbury can be seen across the top of the picture with the cathedral faintly visible just left-of-centre.

STURRY AND FORDWICH [177604] [3-6-56 ?]

A very interesting, and early, photograph of two Stour-side villages — Fordwich, to the top of the picture, and Sturry. The Great Stour flows across the view from near the top-left corner diagonally downwards. The railway runs across the bottom-left corner.

CANTERBURY   [152577] [29-6-49]

A very early view of Canterbury, still showing evidence of damage sustained in the air-raids of the Second World War. The cathedral dominates the centre of the picture, of course, but many changes have since been made to the streets that surround it.

CANTERBURY   [145592] [13-6-67]

A panoramic and rather more distant view looking south-east, showing the rebuilt city centre twenty years on and the spread of the modern suburbs. For all its growth, Canterbury remains, essentially, an attractive country town.

CANTERBURY – UNIVERSITY OF KENT   [141598] [10-7-72]

When seen from the air, the University of Kent at Canterbury looks quite striking on its hilltop setting overlooking the city.

CHILHAM   [068534] [7-7-71]

Chilham has retained much of its medieval atmosphere, as seen from this view. New developments have been kept well away from the ancient centre of the village. The church is situated just above centre with the village square below and the castle just below centre.

BRIDGE [183541] [3-6-56]

Looking north-west along the old A2, Watling Street, long before the construction of the present bypass, towards Canterbury. The church steeple can be seen poking through the trees near the centre of the picture.

BISHOPSBOURNE [188527] [16-6-76]

Bishopsbourne has hardly grown at all since the Middle Ages and remains a delightfully small village. The crop marks to the top of the picture may mark the site of a previous settlement on the opposite bank of the tiny Nailbourne stream.

WHITSTABLE [085645] [29-6-73]

Panorama looking north-east towards the harbour (centre). Whitstable Castle stands on the wooded hill just to the right of the harbour, with Tankerton beyond. The eastern edge of Seasalter occupies the bottom-left corner of the picture.

CHESTFIELD [134652] [7-7-71]

Panorama looking north over Chestfield to Long Rock, the light area in the sea. Tankerton lies to the top-left of the picture, with the holiday camps of Swalecliffe to the right, along the coast.

HERNE BAY [155680] [4-6-65 ?]

Looking east from Hampton Pier (lower left corner) to the pavilion on the main pier before its recent destruction, caused by a fire in 1970 and a gale in 1979. Laid out largely in Victorian times, the town has a very spacious and airy atmosphere. The railway station can be seen near the top-right corner.

RECULVER [228694] [19-7-49]

This early view of Reculver shows the beginnings of what have now become extensive caravan parks. The ruins of a Norman church, with its distinctive towers which act as an aid to shipping, sit within the remains of a Roman fort, clearly defined here. The coastguard cottages near the towers have since become derelict.

SARRE [262652] [1-6-73]

Sarre used to be a thriving port on the Thanet side of the Wantsum Channel. It is now a pleasant village with a disused windmill (situated just below the village on the edge of the fields). The banks of the Wantsum are marked approximately by the road to Monkton, on the left side of the picture. The crop marks may show the former extent of Sarre before it shrank to village status.

BIRCHINGTON [288688] [14-6-61]

Looking out to sea over the western fringes of Birchington to Minnis Bay. Largely built up in modern times, the interest value of this photograph lies in the crop marks and ring ditches in the fields, which may mark the site of a much more ancient settlement.

MARGATE   [356689] [4-6-73]

Panorama looking north, showing the railway station far-left, with the former Dreamland amusement park to the right of that. The harbour is near the centre of the picture, alongside the now demolished pier which was damaged in a storm in 1978. The clearly defined line running from the station to the bottom-right corner is the now dismantled railway that formerly went directly to Ramsgate.

RAMSGATE   [384640] [13-6-67]

The entirely man-made harbour at Ramsgate is very impressive when seen from the air. This view is taken looking north-east across Dumpton to the North Foreland lighthouse. By following the coastline round from the harbour it is possible to locate Bleak House, at Broadstairs.

WINGHAM   [243574] [14-6-61]

Looking north-east towards Ash. Wingham has grown to the status of a small town over the years, but at its heart it is essentially still a village. The road cutting across the upper-left corner follows the line of the Roman road to Ash.

SANDWICH   [332583] [29-6-49]

The clearly defined earthworks of the medieval town wall show to good effect in this early view of Sandwich. So too does the River Stour, which follows an irregular course on the bed of what was once the Wantsum Channel.

GOODNESTONE [259540] [11-6-73]

Looking north-west towards Wingham with the church at the top-centre of the picture and Goodnestone House top-left. Again, there are some interesting crop marks in the fields outside the village which may mark the site of a former settlement.

AYLESHAM   [232514] [11-6-73 ?]

These very interesting crop marks are situated in the fields between Womenswold and Aylesham. The industrial estate occupies the upper-centre with the village itself top-right. The edge of Aylesham Woods can be seen upper-left.

NONINGTON [252525] [11-6-73]

Looking south-east towards Barfreston. The church is situated in the upper-centre of the photograph and, once again, some interesting crop marks are to be seen in the adjacent fields. Despite coal mining activity in the area, Nonington has retained its attractive village centre.

DEAL [377520] [29-6-49]

Looking along the seafront at Deal the sexfoil plan of the castle is easily discernible. The 18th/19th century Governor's House, shown here on the right-most inner bastion, suffered damage in the last war and has since been removed. Some of Deal's extensive barrack buildings can be seen in the lower-left corner.

ST. MARGARET'S AT CLIFFE   [365432] [10-7-72]

The coastal scenery along the South Foreland looks spectacular when viewed from the sea (facing north-west). Much of the area is now protected by the National Trust. St. Margaret's at Cliffe church can be seen just left-of-centre, about a quarter of the way down the picture.

DOVER CASTLE   [327418] [10-7-72]

The magnificent fortifications of Dover Castle span several millennia. The keep, central fortifications and encircling walls date from Norman times, with Napoleonic additions, whilst the horse-shoe shaped earthwork (right of centre) which is itself an Iron Age hillfort, encircles a Saxon church and Roman lighthouse.

DOVER   [327418] [26-6-48]

An early view of Dover showing the Eastern Docks before their development into a major ferry port.
Several of the buildings in the centre of the town still show signs of damage from air-raids in the last war.

STOWTING   [127420] [24-6-54]

From the ground the clump of trees in the centre of the photograph looks insignificant, but here it can be seen as a circular mound. It represents the earthwork remains of Stowting Castle.

FOLKESTONE [234355] [4-6-76]

From the air Folkestone harbour has an attractive and distinctly Continental atmosphere, while the cobbled streets behind remind one of the West Country.

FOLKESTONE WARREN   [252378] [26-6-48]

The coastal scenery at the Warren is dramatically beautiful, especially when seen from the viewpoint. Its present appearance is due to a number of landslips in the area. Capel-le-Ferne, on top of the cliffs, has grown considerably since this view was taken.

SALTWOOD CASTLE   [163358] [26-6-48]

The secluded and partly restored remains of Saltwood Castle, on the hills above Hythe, attracted many visitors even in 1948. The plot to murder Thomas Becket was hatched behind its walls and it survives today as one of the finest Norman castles in the south-east.

LYMPNE [119345] [24-5-76]

The present village lies mostly to the north of the old centre, which is dominated by the church and castle. They used to stand at the head of a coastal cliff but the sea has long-since retreated. Just visible in the lower-left corner are the tumbled remains of a Roman fort.

DYMCHURCH [099291] [26-6-48]

Looking north-east along the coast and over Romney Marsh, this photograph of Dymchurch was taken before its development as a seaside town. A number of 19th century Martello Towers are to be seen along the coastal edge. The church is just visible in the clump of trees in the centre of the main settlement.

LYDD [043210] [2-7-55]

Despite being hemmed in on all sides by military and gravel workings, Lydd remains an attractive place, perhaps more so 30 years ago, when this view was taken, than today. The church can be seen just right-of-centre and, a little way above that, are the tiny triangular remains of the village green.

NEW ROMNEY [068257] [19-7-49]

As its name suggests, New Romney is of newer foundation than its near neighbour, Old Romney, but even this can now be regarded as an ancient settlement. The church used to stand near the old coastline and the new housing estate (now much enlarged) is on land that was once a small harbour.

OLD ROMNEY   [032253] [19-7-49]

The sea has retreated still further from the more ancient settlement of Old Romney. Unlike New Romney, however, which has survived and grown beyond its medieval status, Old Romney has shrunk to a handful of houses surrounding what is now an outsized church.

DUNGENESS [088185] [2-7-55]

Looking south over the shingle ridges at Dungeness before the construction of the controversial nuclear power station, which would occupy the top-right corner of this view. More of a moonscape than a landscape, this apparently barren wilderness has a unique fascination.

WYE [054465] [16-6-76]

Looking north along the wide main street to the rather squat parish church. To the right are the extensive buildings of Wye College. The old centre of this former village can be seen surrounded by more recent buildings, which have elevated Wye to the status of a small town.

CHARING [953493] [29-6-53]

An early view of Charing looking north-east before improvements to the A20 by-passed the village. The church stands out prominently towards the top of the photograph with, beside it, the impressive remains of the Archbishop's Palace.

ASHFORD [997407] [7-7-71]

This modern housing estate in the Stanhope area of Ashford has an almost surrealistic appearance, standing out harshly against the surrounding landscape.

ASHFORD RAILWAY WORKS   [018415] [19-7-49]

Part of the extensive railway works at Ashford. The town centre has seen many changes since this photograph was taken, the Stour Centre now dominating the level area between the River Stour and the railway station, at the top of the picture.

READY TO TEAR

Paper Fashions of the 60s

Jonathan Walford

Library and Archives Canada Cataloguing in Publication

Walford, Jonathan
      Ready to tear : paper fashions of the 1960s / Jonathan Walford.

Includes bibliographical references.

ISBN 978-0-9782230-0-7

      1. Paper garments – History. 2. Fads. 3. Nineteen sixties. I. Title.

TT557.W35 2007   391'.2
C2007-901216-7

Book design: Sohowest Graphicworks sohowest@interlog.com

Published by: Kickshaw Productions www.kickshawproductions.com

Printed in Canada

READY TO TEAR

Paper Fashions of the 60s

In 1966, paper entered a new realm. Not only was the fashion paper dress disposable, and easily alterable, it was a canvas for the 'happening' art scene. Op Art and Super-graphics were applied as easily as psychedelic paisley and flower power prints. And in the days before T-shirt art, the paper dress was the fashion billboard. Advertising products or political candidates, the paper dress was the perfect medium for the message. Paper clothing may have seemed like a space age idea at the time, after all, the 1960s weren't about the past, they were about the future, and what else was the space generation going to wear in lunar cities? Disposable paper clothing of course!

However, there had been an established use of paper for making fashions dating back centuries before the self-consciously modern 1960s came along. From its origins to its popular and revolutionary use, then sudden disappearance, the paper dress evoked so much media coverage at the height of its popularity that few thought it would ever go away.

3

The word paper is derived from the name of the reedy papyrus plant that grows abundantly along the Nile River in Egypt. Sliced sections of the flower stem were pressed and dried into membrane-like sheets for use as writing scrolls by the ancient Egyptians over four thousand years ago. About two thousand years ago, the Chinese discovered that paper could be made from pulped cellulose fibres. The fibres interlocked when wet, bonding into a flat sheet of paper when dried. The Arabs learned the secret of paper making from the Chinese in the twelfth century and the first European paper, milled from cotton and linen rags, was made in 1270 in Fabriano, Italy.

The practical application of typeset printing during the late fifteenth century greatly increased the need for a steady supply of paper. The eighteenth century development of the daily newspaper and the popular novel added to the demand and paper shortages resulted. By 1820, improvements in machinery made the mass production of paper more lucrative but increasing demand put a heavy strain on rag supplies. Canadian Charles Fenerty was the first to create paper from spruce wood pulp in 1838. Unable to find financial backing to secure his invention, other papermakers developed his process. By 1870 large quantities of affordable wood pulp paper were being made in Europe and North America.

Historically, the Chinese and Japanese were the first to use paper for apparel including parasols, fans, hats, masks, and even shoes. Europeans borrowed the idea of the folding fan from the Far East in the seventeenth century. These fans were made with ivory or bone sticks and leafs of paper or silk, often artfully painted. By the mid eighteenth century a stiff heavy paper that was decoratively stamped with patterns was being cut and sewn into hats and bonnets. Known as 'bonnet board', this early form of cardboard was not any less expensive than straw and predated the more practical use of cardboard for packaging but import duties on straw millinery gave cause for the use of 'bonnet board' for fashion headwear. Its use continued well into the nineteenth century. Another style of paper millinery was developed from plaiting strips of newsprint. This technique was undertaken as a craft and was used for making bonnets, handbags and other novel items.

Paper dresses for May Day, Ladies Home Journal, May 1913

A novel example of using paper to create a costume appeared in the circa 1895 edition of the English publication 'Fancy Dresses Described'. It suggests a costume made up of cloth to resemble a wastepaper basket with "...the trimmings being entirely confined to waste paper, which should be sewn with some skill round the hem forming the sleeves and cap."

Anne Fletcher in crepe paper fancy dress, Hamilton, Ontario, c. 1904, courtesy of Whitehern Historic House & Garden, City of Hamilton

English 'bonnet board' paper bonnet, c. 1812 trimmed with blue satin ribbons

German bone and paper fan with painted scene of a garden promenade, c. 1690

Further uses for paper apparel developed at costume parties during the nineteenth century. Fancy dress balls originated during the seventeenth century at carnivals held in the weeks leading up to Lent. Participants would don fancy costumes and wear masks for anonymity but these masked events led to informal behavior and flirtations often turned into trysts. Masquerades fell from favour in the early nineteenth century as a more restrained society adopted a higher moral tone but the love of fancy dress did not diminish. Fancy dress parties during the nineteenth century placed more emphasis on the costumes and paper was often employed in the creation of elaborate fancy dresses. An article that appeared in the Toronto newspaper The Evening Telegram on May 6, 1936 recounted an event that had happened in that city in 1876:

"Sixty years ago Miss Ida Romain, a belle of early Toronto, created a sensation with a remarkable costume made entirely of newspaper, which she wore to a fancy dress ball given on behalf of the Protestant Orphan's Home. Miss Romain made it herself with the aid of a seamstress, sewing the newspapers firmly to stiff buckram, and cleverly fashioning frills for the voluminous skirt and tight bodice… she even contrived a newspaper bouquet

American Crepe paper Halloween dress, hat, and mask, c. mid 1920s

Suggestions for fancy dress costumes available in kits from Reed's, including butterfly, tulip, and harlequin, c. 1920

Dennison store advertising board for crepe paper costumes, American, mid 1930s. From the 1910s until the 1950s, crepe paper was the popular and affordable material choice for fancy dress costumes. Eventually plastic and other inexpensive synthetic materials found more favour, primarily for their waterproof qualities.

Crepe paper how-to booklet, 1921

Reed's crepe paper daisy outfit kit, c. 1920

holder… A Toronto newspaper account of the ball had this to say of Miss Romain's dress "The attire worn by Miss Romain was remarkable for its novelty. It consisted of a complete dress and overskirt with panniers made of issues of the city press with the names of the three daily papers published in the city conspicuous on the front of the over-skirt. Miss Romain's partners could easily read the news of the day while enjoying the whirlings of the gallopade."

Paper costumes got a boost in the 1890s when a technique for making crepe paper was developed. Crepe paper had elastic qualities, and could be sewn to textiles and manipulated to resemble frills. Suggestions for wearing a spring fashion frock of paper appeared in the May 1913 Ladies Home Journal.

Crepe paper child's costume, Canadian, c. late 1930s

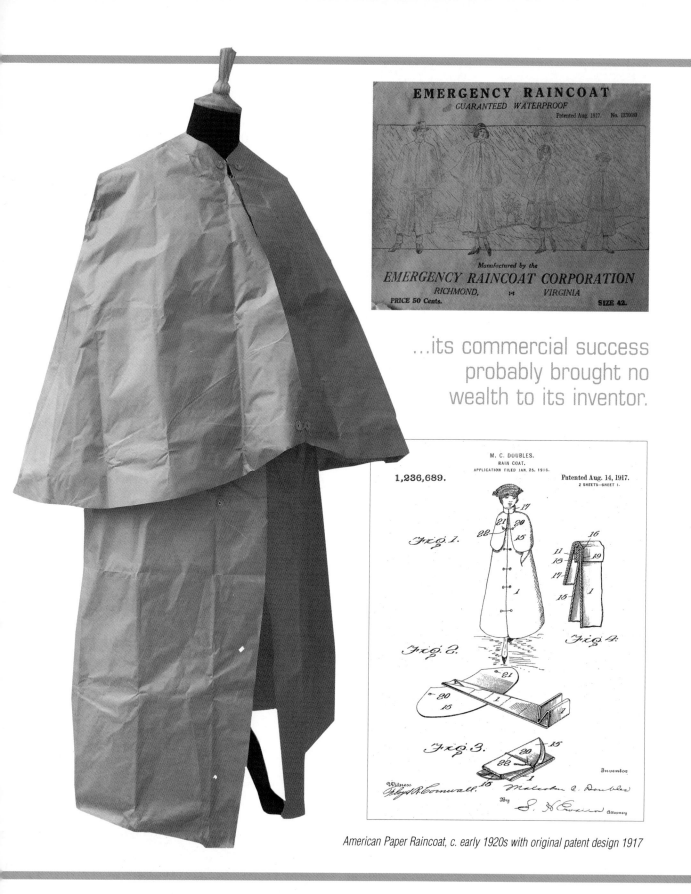

...its commercial success probably brought no wealth to its inventor.

American Paper Raincoat, c. early 1920s with original patent design 1917

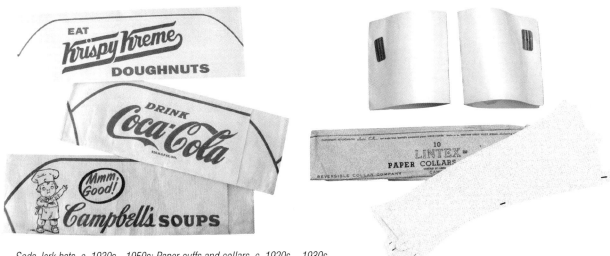

Soda Jerk hats, c. 1930s - 1950s; Paper cuffs and collars, c. 1920s – 1930s

"These costumes may be made at home by any girl who wants a floral dress for May Day…They are equally appropriate for fancy dress parties of any kind. The cost of the costumes and hats ranges from $1.03 to $1.70 for materials… This amount, however, does not include the Princesse slip which is used as a foundation. This may be purchased at any department store for 75 cents… The paper is sewed to the slip with mercerized thread, while paste is used for appliqué work."

As Halloween became an annual costumed event during the early twentieth century in North America, partygoers transformed themselves into flowers, pixies or gypsies with the brightly coloured crepe paper sewn onto plain cotton underclothes. Although crepe paper was notorious for dye bleeds the cotton undergarment to which it was sewn was guaranteed to retain propriety and besides, the whole idea was that the costume would only be worn for one occasion. The crepe paper costume was seen as fun, inexpensive and disposable, and became a Halloween staple until the 1950s.

The first appearance of paper fashions for daily wear appeared in Germany during World War I when blockades had disrupted the importation of textiles. The English publication West End Gazette reported in November 1915 that "dresses and suits of paper have been sold in enormous quantities in Berlin, and they are warm and keep out the rain remarkably well." No known examples of German paper clothing from 1915 survive so what these looked like is pure conjecture. An American patent for a brown paper raincoat was granted in 1917. Made of Kraft paper with string toggle closures, the cloak was stiff and although marketed for emergency use, its commercial success probably brought no wealth to its inventor.

In Germany by 1916, cotton was nearly unattainable for civil purposes. The German textile industry experimented with reeds and nettle fibers but it was wood pulp yarn that proved particularly resistant and durable. Woven cloth made of wood pulp yarn could be woven, dyed, printed, and sewn into garments and underwear. However, in October 1917, the Prussian war ministry department for raw materials even confiscated wood pulp yarn for military use. This German development mirrored the invention of rayon viscose.

As early as 1855 French processes for making threads from wood pulp were being experimented with but the first practicable development in rayon viscose did not happen until 1905 in England. Rayon, or artificial silk as it was then known, did not become commercially viable until the early 1920s and although its base material is wood pulp it is a synthesized yarn and is woven into cloth and therefore does not constitute the definition of paper, which is pressed rather than woven.

Paper entered into the realm of utilitarian household products in the 1920s. A new absorbent paper for use as bandages, intended to replace cotton wool, was first processed in the United States during World War I. Nurses found it useful for menstruation and in 1920 Kotex became the first brand to market paper menstrual pads. Paper tissues were first sold in 1924 under the brand name of Kleenex. Originally intended for removing cold cream from the face, users of Kleenex discovered them to be more useful and hygienic as disposable handkerchiefs.

Paper was again used for millinery in the 1920s. Decoratively printed crepe and heavy tissue paper was fashioned into wide brimmed hats and instruction booklets on how to craft your own sporty crocheted crepe paper cloches appeared in the mid 1920s. Disposability and cost were factors in the advancement of paper apparel in the 1920s and 1930s. As an alternative to heavily starched linen or cotton collars and cuffs, paper ones were especially beneficial for men who traveled and didn't want to carry around dirty laundry or deal with having laundry done while away from home. Restaurant workers donned hats as part of their uniform for hygienic reasons and disposable paper hats started being provided by suppliers who took the opportunity to advertise their product on the sides of the crowns. By the late 1920s every corner drug store that had a soda fountain had an employee known as a soda jerk and his hat, which was based on a military wedge cap (also known as a forage or garrison cap), became identified as a soda jerk hat.

American Rose print black striped crepe paper hat, c. early 1920s

CROCHET HATS ARE THE SMARTEST VOGUE OF THE SEASON

Just imagine it, the materials for any of these chic models cost less than $2.00, including the Crepe Paper, Wire and Ribbon for the Trimming

American brochure on how to make crepe paper hats, 1922

Illustration of crocheted crepe paper hats, promoted as suitable for summer sportswear, 1923

The demand for paper products dropped as the Depression took its toll on the pulp and paper industry in the 1930s. The commercial success of artificial silk, renamed rayon in 1924 set the textile industry in motion to create new forms of synthetic fibres. Advancements in the use of paper floundered as cellophane, neoprene and nylon took over textile industry news headlines. Paper wasn't completely abandoned however as paper was still used for partygoers at fancy dress paper balls. One of the most famous of the period was held at the Wadsworth Athenaeum museum in Hartford, Connecticut in 1936. The paper dress code required all attendees to use paper in the creation of their party attire and while many invitees opted for only a minimal use of paper, some party-goers went all out for the grand entrance parade which consisted of a huge variety of paper animals, shepherdesses and other characters.

Paper began making headway again in the late 1940s. Disposable menstrual pads had been marketed since 1920 but nobody thought of using the same technology for making diapers. Paper diapers were first made in Sweden during the Second World War but this was the result of paper being used as a substitute material due to cotton being in short supply. With the first wave of the Baby Boom making its impact, Eastern Airlines commissioned Chicopee Paper Mills to develop a disposable paper diaper with plastic outer layer to help passengers who traveled with babies on transatlantic flights. The result was the CHUX disposable diaper, first made in 1949. Disposable paper diapers were a luxury and not used by most mothers but for emergency occasions outside the home. However, they were now a convenience that grew in popularity, eventually becoming considered a necessity for all occasions by the 1970s. Although diapers are not a fashion statement, their introduction revitalized interest in exploring paper as a convenient, inexpensive and disposable product that had possibilities of expansive use.

American comic postcard, c. 1940

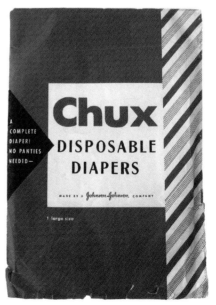

Chux disposable diaper, c. 1950

A FAB, MAD, MOD, FAD

COLOR EXPLOSION FLASHES INTO FASHION WITH THE PAPER DRESS! $1

It's the "Paper Caper" by Scott. What a conversation piece! Clip the coupon below, mail it with your money for the dress that is now!

GET A SCOTT

Paper Caper DRESS

THE SCOTT PAPER CAPER. IT'S A PAPER DRESS WEAR IT FOR KICKS — THEN GIVE IT THE AIR

Send $1.25 along with two front panels from any of the Scott Bathroom tissues — PUREX, SCOTTISSUE, LAD... SCOTT or CASHMERE. Indicate your size & colour choic... & mail to:

**SCOTT PAPER CAPER
BOX 2195
TORONTO, ONTARIO**

Please send me _____ Scott Paper Capers.
I enclose $ _____ and _____ Scott bathroom tiss... labels. Offer expires Dec. 31, 1966.

CHECK YOUR SIZE	BANDANA		OP-ART	
	LARGE	SMALL		LARGE	SMA...
	MEDIUM	PETITE		MEDIUM	PET...

(Sizes: Petite 3 to 6, Small 7 to 10, Medium 11-14, Large 15-...

NAME _____
ADDRESS _____
CITY _____ PROV. _____

VOIR AU VERSO

The disposability and cost advantages of th new paper material was originally intended for use in hospitals and laboratories.

12

n April 1966, the Scott Paper Company promoted a new line of decoratively printed-paper towels called "Colorful Explosions". With a mail-in order coupon and one dollar, plus 25 cents for shipping and handling, anyone could order one of two styles of printed-paper dresses by mail. Much to their surprise, Scott filled nearly half a million orders by year's end. The paper dress craze had been launched!

The paper used in the dresses was made of a rayon scrim sandwiched between two layers of cellulose fibre. According to the June 16, 1967 issue of Parade magazine, the St. Regis Paper Company invented the scrim-strengthened paper in the 1950s, but they did not produce it. The American companies of Scott and Kimberly-Stevens began making the reinforced paper as early as 1958. Scott made the paper using a rayon mesh and Kimberly-Stevens used a nylon mesh, both of which used a ratio of 93% cellulose to 7% synthetic scrim. The disposability and cost advantages of this new paper material was originally intended for use in hospitals and laboratories but there had been talk within the industry about using the paper for clothes, tablecloths, and other household textiles.

The manufacturers were concerned about how to market their material. They didn't want to overstate its qualities nor underrate its possibilities. Kimberly-Stevens did not want to call the material 'paper' thinking consumers would reject it for lack of durability. Generically, the manufacturers referred to the material as a 'disposable' or 'non-woven' product. Scott called its paper product 'Dura-weave' and Kimberly-Stevens trademarked their nylon scrim material 'Kaycel' following the tradition of calling their products by names beginning with the letter 'K', as they had done with Kleenex and Kotex.

In 1965, Robert Bayer, an engineer working with Scott Paper had his wife design a simple A-line

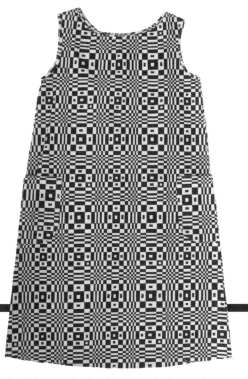 

Promotional photograph, advertisement, order form and paper dresses from Scott paper, 1966. These two designs launched the fad for paper clothing in the late 1960s.

WASTE BASKET BOUTIQUE ™

MARS OF ASHEVILLE

THE PIONEER IN DISPOSABLE FASHION

dress for making paper dress samples to sell to department stores. No interest could be stirred until after Scott launched its paper dress promotion in the spring of 1966. Scott called its red and yellow bandanna and black and white Op Art print dresses 'Paper Caper' and advertised the benefits of its reinforced triple-ply paper material that came with a warning attached to every dress or package that washing would remove fire retardants:

"To shorten the paper dress, all that is needed is a steady hand and a pair of scissors. To mend it, sticky tape is dandy… While you should not count on more than one wearing, depending on use many have been able to get three or four wearings from a Paper Caper dress. You can also cut up the dress for using as disposable guest towels, placements or an apron… It will never displace that little black dress as a wardrobe staple, but as a conversation piece, as an attention attraction, the Paper Caper is unique."

As a sponsor of the televised Junior Miss Pageant in 1966, Scott previewed its dresses on the nationwide broadcast and in April the promotion was launched in the United States. The Canadian launch followed in August. By year's end, despite the nearly half million dresses sold by Scott, they had made little money from direct sales as they had sold the dresses for near cost. However, upon hearing of the success of the Scott dresses, the

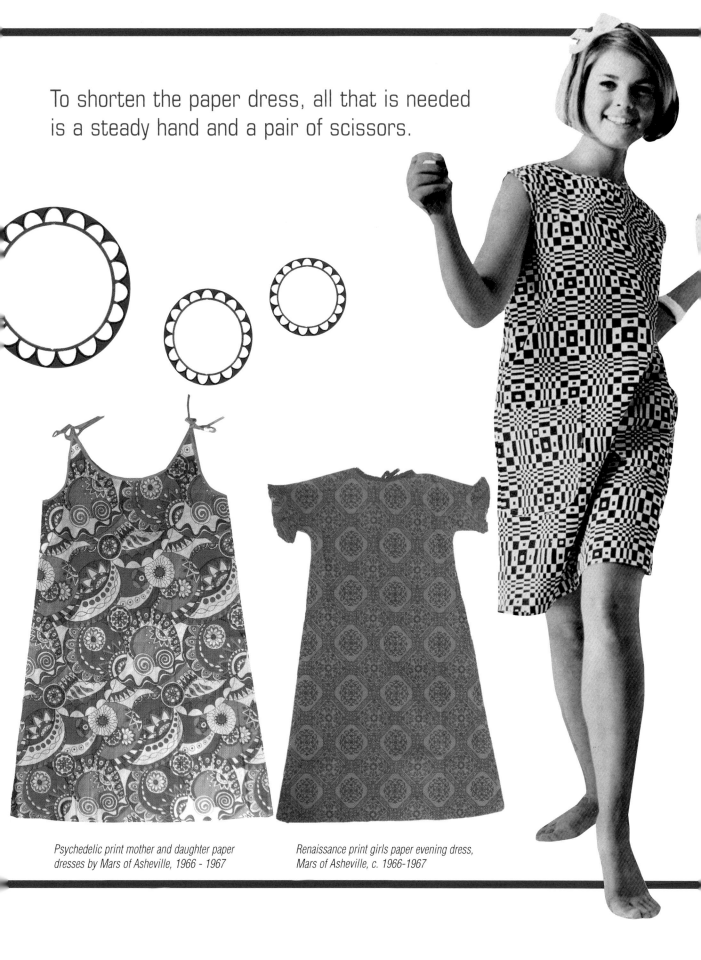

To shorten the paper dress, all that is needed is a steady hand and a pair of scissors.

Psychedelic print mother and daughter paper dresses by Mars of Asheville, 1966 - 1967

Renaissance print girls paper evening dress, Mars of Asheville, c. 1966-1967

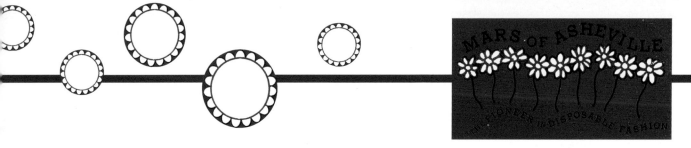

"Five years from now 75% of the nation will be wearing disposable clothing" - Ronald Bard, Vice president of Mars (1966)

media jumped on the story and a flood of commentary appeared on the subject. The publicity the dresses brought Scott far surpassed their wildest dreams. The initial reports were overwhelmingly positive, and went beyond the company's own marketing strategy. The Seattle Post Intelligencer, reported on June 14, 1966 "Wear the shift and then toss it away. No washing helps take care of water shortage."

Despite its success, Scott had no intentions of continuing the paper dress venture in 1967. In an interview with R.T. Stewart, a marketing director for

Scott Paper Ltd., The Toronto newspaper The Globe and Mail reported on February 21, 1967 "the use of paper clothing could be a fad that will die out. Durable clothing could be made of paper but the price is relatively high for items that in most cases are thrown away after one wearing." A Kimberly-Stevens representative agreed in the article and felt that the bulk of its paper fabric production was in the industrial and institutional fields. The same newspaper had reported earlier, on June 9, 1966 that two major studies were almost complete in Michigan and California hospitals for cost efficiency

Mars of Asheville printed-paper dresses with variety of strap, neckline and sleeve styles, 1966 – 1968

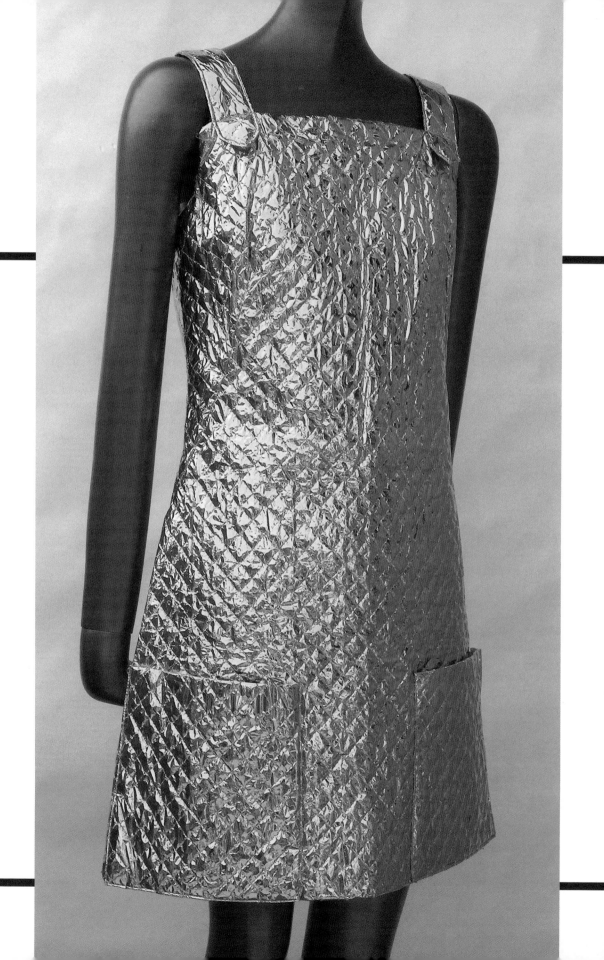

Green Foil paper dress by Mars of Asheville, Silver Foil paper dress by Beau Monde, New Jersey, Blue quilted foil paper dress, unlabelled, probably Mars of Asheville, 1966 – 1967

By September of 1966, Mars of Asheville was shipping sleeveless shift dresses to J.C. Penny that retailed for $1.29, sleeved and floor length dresses retailed higher. Foil paper dresses that Mars said was used to insulate space suits created a stir that autumn as well, with short versions selling for $6.00 and evening gowns selling for $9.00. Special disposable clothing shops sprang up,

and stores that carried unique designer items expanded their merchandise to include paper dresses. "In Dispensable Disposables", "Paperworks", and "Paraphernalia" were well known Manhattan haunts that carried the hippest paper clothing available. Major high-end department stores were also carrying paper dresses that fall including J.R. Robinson in Los Angeles, and Gimbels, Stern Brothers and Abraham and Straus in New York. California's Joseph Magnin & Co., created a special 'News Stand" boutique in twenty-eight of its stores.

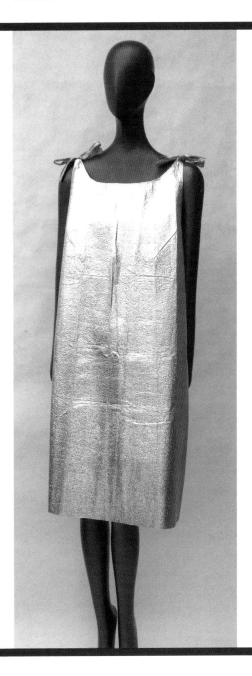

between disposables and laundering but that laundering was still slightly cheaper. However, with an increase in production of paper bedding, the cost was expected to fall. Toronto's The Financial Post reported on September 17, 1966, "(industrial) garments are all uncomplicated. Their utility is high, fashion low, and cutting and sewing operations minimal… Within a decade all industrial firms with jobs that soil clothing will be using disposable protective garments."

The manufacturers were not optimistic about the future of paper fashion despite the sensational media coverage and public response to the $1.25 paper frocks. However, the self-consciously modern 1960s and its optimistic quest for a space-age future had created a progress-minded society that was ready to embrace the ephemeral quality of dispos-able apparel. The New York Times reported on September 6, 1966 that paper fabric shifts were appearing on the streets

Zebra print pantsuit with matching hat by James Sterling Fashions, New York. This was James Sterling's most popular design and was available from late spring 1966 until 1968.

Psychedelic zodiac animal print evening dress by James Sterling, c. 1966-1967

JAMES STERLING PAPER FASHIONS, LTD
200 MADISON AVENUE • SUITE 1904
NEW YORK, N.Y., 10016

PANT SUIT AND HAT
Black & White
jungle print,

Can be pressed with
cool iron.
Flame proof unles...
Soft, strong, drap...
To shorten, cut...
scissors.

More manufacturers were stepping into the disposable apparel market. James Sterling of New York was producing $7.50 zebra print pantsuits, $15.00 bridal gowns, and $8.00 maternity dresses as well as a cheaper line sold through Sears Roebuck & Co. Sterling felt the best market for paper clothing was in resort wear. Vacationers could buy paper clothes at the hotel when they arrived and throw them away when they departed, thus eliminating packing and carrying luggage. Formfit Rogers, an underwear manufacturer sold a $3.00 paper ensemble intended for travelers that included a bra, petti-skirt and kerchief. Mars of Asheville was also developing its market to include disposable underwear, which they felt had a permanent place in clothing sales, especially for travelers.

of New York. This statement gave paper dresses credibility – if paper dresses were being worn in New York then it must be fashion!

In a joint venture with Kimberly-Stevens, the makers of Kaycel paper, the North Carolina hosiery manufacturer Mars of Asheville went into the paper dress market purely as a fashion enterprise. Kimberly provided the paper in plain white rolls and a gift-wrap company was contracted to print a variety of patterns, including awning stripe and marbleized designs in several colour-ways. The new line was launched under the label 'Waste Basket Boutique' and hit the market in June of 1966. The most avid industry representative of paper dress futures was Ronald Bard, Vice president of Mars. On September 6, 1966 The New York Times quoted him as saying "Five years from now 75% of the nation will be wearing disposable clothing" Years later in a Newsday article that appeared in 1999, Bard admitted he was convinced in 1966 that by 1980 half of all clothing would be made from non-woven products. Julian Tomshin, a textile designer who became fascinated with the paper apparel phenomena was quoted in the November 25, 1966 issue of LIFE magazine stating "It's right for our age, after all who is going to do laundry in space?" Tomshin believed that improved techniques would bring prices down until garments would be packaged in tear-off rolls, like sandwich bags and sold for pennies in vending machines. However, retailers were less enthusiastic about the domination of paper clothing in the future. Most were quoted as being open to the idea that paper clothing was a great gag for summer fun but that it would never overtake the tradition of silk or wool clothing. The Financial Post reported on September 17, 1966 "Where they can compete economically consumers will buy paper garments that retail less than the cost of laundering or dry cleaning cloth garments, or offer greater convenience by being disposable."

No need to worry that such a democratic dress... one that absolutely anyone can afford - will destroy the fashion elite.

The Wadsworth Athenaeum had held a famous paper ball in 1936 and in late 1966 decided it was time to host another paper party. Society commentator Marilyn Bender wrote at the time "No need to worry that such a democratic dress - one that absolutely anyone can afford - will destroy the fashion elite. The woman of wealth and social contacts can commission an artist to create a special paper dress for a special event, then donate it to a museum, provided the garment hasn't deteriorated on the dance floor." The Hartford Connecticut museum proved this point. Instead of cheap and cheerfully disposable paper frocks, designers were hired to create unique couture creations for the event. Three examples of hand painted gowns by New York designer Tzaims Luksus cost a thousand dollars each and were featured in the November 25 issue of LIFE magazine. The dresses became part of Wadsworth's permanent collection. The Valley Stream synagogue held a similar fund-raiser ball with a paper dress code, and in 1967, a paper dress ball held in New York included one guest who wore a Bill Blass creation of cheetah-print paper trimmed with sable. A fundraising event in Washington D.C. in 1967 took a different approach by having guests trade in their couture clothes for auctioning, receiving a paper dress to wear home.

Designers were now in on the trend and none was more active than Elisa Daggs of New York who created paper garments for sixty department stores including Bonwit Teller and Lord & Taylor. Daggs had come from a background of fashion magazine editing for Harper's Bazaar, Vogue, Charm and Bride's magazines. Her striped kaftans, waterproofed paper raincoats and bikinis were not intended for those who liked

Mars of Asheville paper dress with felt tip marker painted design of women with flowing hair signed Schaldeman, c. 1966 - 1967; Child's paper dress and paint kit, Mars of Asheville, c. 1966-1967; Mars of Asheville paper dress with silk screened 'fragile' design by Andy Warhol, September, 1966, photo courtesy of the Brooklyn Museum of Art.

Warhol silk-screened "Fragile" onto the front of his plain white paper dress while the model was wearing it and signed his work "Dali".

The Brooklyn based Abraham and Straus was the first major department store to carry paper dresses beginning in late June of 1966 and by September had reported sales of three thousand paper dresses as well as practical paper aprons and make-up capes. To launch a special street level paper boutique in September, Abraham and Straus staged a 'happening' to promote a new product line from Mars of Asheville – plain white dresses that came with watercolour paint sets for 'doing your own thing'. Andy Warhol, who was commissioned to promote the new line at the event, silk-screened "Fragile" onto the front of his plain white paper dress while a model was wearing it and signed his work "Dali". To commemorate the event, Abraham and Strauss donated Warhol's wearable art dress to the Brooklyn Museum.

Hand-painted dresses commissioned from New York designer Tzaimus Luksus for the Wadsworth Athenaeum ball were featured in Life magazine, May 1966. Photo courtesy of Howell Conant.

the cheap aspect of paper clothing. Her quest was to make paper clothing chic, desirable to those at the top end of the market. The Seattle Post Intelligencer quoted her on May 25, 1967: "Let's get one thing straight right away – A disposable dress is a luxury. It is not for the poor. Only people with money can afford to buy things to use a few times and throw away... Much of the new paper material is fireproof but then it can't be cleaned or washed. There is no use trying to approach this from a practical standpoint. You have to have fun with it, in a riot of color. I think my place is that I have added the fashion element. I haven't gooked the clothes up with buttons or zippers. They all work as simply as an envelope. They wrap, tie, and they are all made in one size with expandable sides or back... Paper clothes won't die. Just by the nature of the material, they create a new fashion architecture but until they can be made by fusing or molding instead of being cut and sewn – five or six years from now, maybe – there is no point at all in treating them as anything but what they are: Expensive fun."

Similarly, Judith Brewer, a California designer with a boutique in Beverly Hills had been raising the fashion level of the disposable dress, along with its price. Her dresses sold for between ten and forty dollars with a top end price of $200 for a paper fur coat. Bonnie Cashin started creating paper hats,

Elisa Daggs oriental-style wrap coat using Velcro fastenings and a hip belt to close the coat. In keeping with the modern idea of disposable clothing, Velcro was a new form of closure patented by Swiss inventor George de Mestral in 1955 but not used to any great extent in the clothing industry until the mid 1960s.

Within a decade all industrial firms with jobs that soil clothing will be using disposable protective garments.

but by 1968 also had a line of clothes labeled "Bonnie Cashin's Paper-Route to Fashion". British designer Veronica Marsh produced raincoats of PVC laminated paper that had a life expectancy of two to three months, or one season's worth of wear. Paco Rabanne created a paper wedding dress in June of 1967, Even the doyenne with an eye for fashion evils, Mr. Blackwell, designed a paper dress for his 1967 collection.

By the end of 1966, Mars of Asheville was the leading manufacturer in disposables, producing 80,000 garments per week. 1.4 million paper garments had been sold and sales from paper garments amounted to $3.5 million U.S. Projected sales for 1967 topped $6 million but halfway through 1967 projected sales were re-estimated to top $30 million.

Kaycel evening dress by James Sterling Paper Fashions, c. 1967

Newsprint Kaycel paper dress, unlabelled, c. 1967

Paperdelic meditation mini – the guru paper dress – 'wear while sitar listening or just thinking' Argus National Corp, Los Angeles, California, c. 1967

Kaycel beach cover-up by James Sterling Paper Fashions, c. 1967

Introducing The Paper Generation.

Some call today's youth "mod". Others call them "mad". We call them The Paper Generation. Why? Just look at the picture. The girl in the paper dress and paper jewellery is standing beside the boy in the paper fur coat on the paper chair in front of the paper lamp. See? The Paper Generation. The Canadian Pulp and Paper Pavilion at Expo 67 will introduce you to The Paper Generation.

In a dazzling theatrical setting, we'll show you the modern drama of paper in films, cartoons, live stage presentations. We'll show you why, in today's Canada, pulp and paper is rightly called our most spectacular and progressive industry. Just bring a smile and an out— stretched mind. We'll do the rest.

*Paper fashions were highlighted at Canada's Expo '67
in Montreal at the Canadian Pulp and Paper Pavilion*

THE POSSIBILITIES ARE ENDLESS

I n October 1966 Moda Mia, a division of the cosmetics company Rayette-Faberge Inc., launched their line of Mexican print shifts that sold for $1.98 in drug stores and supermarkets. The dresses were made of Fibron, a disposable rayon mesh fabric that had tiny perforations over the entire surface. Fibron was made by Chicopee Mills and was introduced in the 1950s as a limited use kitchen cleaning cloth that could be washed several times before discarding. The cloths were marketed under the brand name 'Handi-wipes' in the United States and 'J-Cloth' in Canada and the U.K. Moda Mia's launch of Fibron may have seemed like a foray into a new alternative disposable material but in reality it was in response to a growing shortage of paper. Scott was focusing on Industrial uses for its Dura-weave and Kimberly-Stevens, who produced Kaycel, already had agreements with buyers for most of its product, primarily Mars of Asheville. There was little surplus to sell to anyone else. The market was truly now more accurately described as 'disposable' rather than 'paper' since cellulose paper products were in serious short supply and alternative disposables were hitting the market.

Parade magazine dealt with the issue of shortages in their June 18, 1967 issue. Ron Bard, the then 25-year-old vice president of Mars of Asheville told Parade "Back in 1963 I wrote my thesis at North Caroline State on the subject of paper. They all laughed. Now about 75 percent of the major department stores carry our line. I've had to turn down premium offers from abroad because of

Moda Mia Mexican print shifts made of Fibron hit the market in October 1966

supply problems." Kimberly-Stevens, the major supplier of the fabric Kaycel had a backlog of orders running into late fall of 1967. Their machines were so busy they were planning on building another plant. A representative from Kimberly-Stevens told Parade that Kaycel was developed over seven years ago but "We offered it in 15 colours, No dice. Today, in plain white only, look at this backlog!" Time magazine quipped in their March 17, 1967 magazine that all customers of Kaycel were now on

"K-rations… Manufacturers are turning to Dupont's Reemay® as an alternative."

Dupont's Reemay® was the other new wonder material that was now being used to make disposable dresses. Made in a process called 'spun-bonded' Reemay® consisted of polyester filaments bonded into position by heat and pressure. The material needed no reinforcing scrim to keep it from tearing, it was machine washable up to a half

'The Little Dipper' Tyvek bathing suit by Fling-Things Inc., Pennsylania, c. 1967

dozen times, lightweight, strong, drape-able, resisted wrinkling, and had an attractive surface with a subtle swirl pattern that showed through the print design. Introduced in 1964, Reemay® was originally intended as an interlining material.

Dupont had also developed Tyvek®, similar in production to Reemay® but made from high-density thermoplastic polyolefin fibres. Kendall Industry made a similar product called Webril. These two products had outstanding toughness and puncture resistance but no porosity. Mars of Asheville had employed Tyvek® in creating disposable swimming trunks in 1966. Sold primarily to hotels and motels that provided them for their guests who had forgotten to pack swimming attire, their only drawback was in trapping air, which could embarrassingly bubble up from under the water's surface. Despite this issue, three thousand were sold within the first year.

By spring 1967 more manufacturers were turning to Reemay®, Fibron, Tyvek® or Webril to produce their disposable clothing. Toronto's The Financial Post printed an article on April 8, 1967, which outlined Canadian dress manufacturer complaints that no mill in Canada was making Kaycel and had to rely on imports from the United States. "Stores across the U.S., particularly in New York have managed to grab enough stock... (but) John Burkholder, owner of Black and White and a Toronto designer used the shops' stock of Kaycel bed sheets to present a collection." Louben Sportswear, the only Canadian volume manufacturer of disposable dresses, had managed to secure enough Kaycel from Kimberly-Stevens but others had to do without. Despite the fact that a growing number of disposable dresses were no longer made of cellulose paper, the popular image identifying disposable garments as being made of paper continued.

By the spring of 1967 the uses of all disposable materials began to break new ground. Mars of Asheville, James Sterling and Day's Sportswear in Tacoma Washington test marketed men's paper pants and suits in 1967. The American artist James Rosenquist made a stir at his pop-art show openings in a paper suit and the Beatles appeared in neon orange paper jackets in Los Angeles during a North American tour, but men were less enthusiastic about paper clothing. Traditional tailoring, required for slacks and jackets, were not profitable manufacturing techniques for paper.

In an attempt to widen the market, twisted paper for use as yarn in making women's hats and handbags showed up in craft stores. Butterick,

McCall and Vogue printed patterns specifically designed for paper. Designs were free form so they needed no facings, armholes were cut deeper to avoid tearing, and neck and sleeve edges were stitched by machine. Joyce Carter, fashion writer for Toronto's Globe Magazine failed to see the advantage of making dresses at home from paper. She wrote in the April 22, 1967 edition "The paper material costs about a dollar a yard in a 45-inch width (but) there are lots of cottons and synthetics available at a dollar a yard, so there's no price cut. If you used the same shortcut techniques, fabric wouldn't take longer to sew and could be washed. Even a keen home sewer will admit that it still takes less time to wash out a garment than to stitch-up a replacement."

'Candy Wrappers' Reemay dress by Mallory Corporation, Dallas Texas, 1968

Reemay evening dress customized by the owner who cut off the bottom of the dress, fringed the strips of material and then applied them to the mini-length dress, no label, c. 1967- 1968

'Almost PaperFashions' beach shift of polyethylene laminated reemay, c. 1968

(left and lower right) Reemay paper dresses by James Sterling Fashions Ltd. for Sears. The packaging boasted 'made with Reemay 100% spunbonded polyester by Dupont - with the look and feel of chiffon - permanently fire retardant, won't fray, ravel or split, strong, drapable, dries in a jiffy, needs no ironing but can be pressed with cool iron., retains its body and shape, long wearing and comfortable because it's a 'breather'.'

Regardless of how some were beginning to feel about the whole fad, others were still looking forward to its future. The California designer Judith Brewer was reported in Time magazine on March 17, 1967 as saying she was looking forward to knit and stretch paper for making stockings and ski pants and that someday paper clothing would be sold in vending machines. However, Toronto's Globe and Mail reported near the beginning of the paper apparel craze on June 9, 1966 "In Stockholm you can buy paper shirts from vending machines for 25 cents each. You can choose white, coloured, or patterned with soft and hard collars."

The Canadian Pulp and Paper Industry showcased the possibilities of the use of paper in their pavilion at Expo 67 in Montreal. Clothes for men and women, shoes, bedspreads, chairs, lamps - the possibilities were endless. Stores like 'Paperworks' in Manhattan offered paper curtains, drapes and sheets. Paper was expanding into new territory when cardboard furniture was being offered at hip stores, most of it being imported from Europe and Scandinavia. In the summer of 1967 a 'Design-in' was organized in New York's Central Park. Participants sat on paper chairs and saw the official launch of the 'Plydom', a 375 square foot paper house designed by Canadian Howard Yates that could be set up in two hours. Designed as a vacation property dwelling, the aluminum frame and accordion pleated laminated paper home had already been test marketed in California to house migrant workers. The laminating process was a breakthrough for the future of paper and the Plydom was being touted as a model for what some day might become lunar housing.

...someday paper clothing would be sold in vending machines

Psychedelic print Reemay shifts, c. 1967 and Reemay pantsuit by Fling Things, Unitex Products, Philadelphia, Pennsylvania, c. 1967

Breck Shampoo premium offer for paper dresses, Seventeen magazine, July 1967

Mars of Asheville Kaycel dress for 20th Century Fox Studios advertising films in production during 1967 including: The Prime of Miss Jean Brodie; The Pilot; The Boston Strangler; A Walk with Love and Death; Che!; Butch Cassidy and the Sundance Kid; Blood and Guts (renamed Patton upon release); The Only Game in Town; Beyond the Valley of the Dolls; Staircase; John Brown's Body; The Chairman; Joanna; Tom Swift; Justine, The Magus, The Gurus; Hello Dolly; Star; The Planet of the Apes Revisited; Lady in Cement; The Touchables; Tora Tora Tora; Myra Breckinridge; The Confession of Nat Turner; 100 Rifles; Hard Contract.

Warhol's pop art style influenced more than just the Campbell's Souper dress of 1967. His style of silk-screen printing found its way onto Universal Studio's 'Big One's of '68' paper dress that featured stars of that studio's leading films in production including: Elizabeth Taylor and Richard Burton in "Go Forth"; Mary Tyler Moore in "What's So Bad About Feeling Good"; George Peppard in "P.J."; Don Knotts in "The Shakiest Gun in the West"; James Garner in "The Jolly Pink Jungle"; Paul Newman in "The Secret War of Harry Frigg"; Oliver Reed in "I'll Never Forget What's 'Is Name"; Shirley Maclaine in "Sweet Charity"; Julie Andrews in "Thoroughly Modern Millie"; Vanessa Redgrave in "Isadora"; Albert Finney in "Charlie Bubbles"; Rod Taylor and Claudia Cardinale in "A Time for Heroes"; Marlon Brando in "The Night of the Following Day"; Richard Widmark and Henry Fonda in "Madigan"; Charlton Heston in "Counterpoint"; Phyllis Diller in "Did You Hear the One About the Traveling Saleslady?"; Kirk Douglas and Sylvia Koscina in "A Lovely Way to Die"; Doris Day in "The Ballad of Josie".

The promotional use of paper clothing flourished. With clips of coupons from magazines, dresses could be bought from a variety of companies. Some offered fashion flower power or psychedelic paisley prints that had no obvious correlation to their business while others chose prints that reflected their product. In the days before T-shirt art marketing executives took advantage of the visual merchandising potential of the paper dress 'billboard'.

Fibron evening dress, available from Viking Kitchen Carpets, American, c. 1967

STEAL THE SCENE IN
VIKING'S KITCHEN PARTY DRESS

Designed by *Andrée*
of New York
Exclusively for
Viking Kitchen Carpets.

Value $6. ONLY $1.
Swinging, disposable hostess
gown made of a miracle
fabric that's tear-resistant
and fire-retardant. Wear it
long. Snip it short. Let your-
self go with bright ideas . . .

See other side.

Campbell's offered what is probably now the most famous paper dress of the era. Re-appropriating Andy Warhol's artistic interpretation of their soup cans, Campbell's produced the "Souper Dress" in the spring of 1967.

Yellow Pages print Reemay dress from Mars of Asheville offered in Parade magazine, October 1968

Kaycel paper dress labeled 'From Time – the Weekly Newsmagazine', c. 1967

Holly and floral printed-paper dresses by Hallmark, American, c. 1967

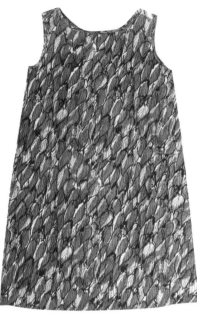

Green leaf print Dura-weave paper dress by Scott, available from Jolly Green Giant, 1967. Although Scott did not seek the fashion market with their Dura-weave paper, Green Giant was one of the few commissions they took on in the late 1960s

In the spring of 1967 Hallmark went into the clothing business when they marketed a complete party kit, including disposable printed shift, matching cups, plates, place mats, napkins, and invitations. Paper dresses for the Hallmark hostess could be bought separately in any store that carried Hallmark stationary products. Mars of Asheville was quick to copy this marketing technique and soon offered a variety of party accessories to coordinate with some of its paper dresses.

Mars of Asheville Kaycel paper dress with three and six inch wide horizontal stripes of pink commissioned by Owens Corning to promote their new 3 and 6 inch pink fiberglass insulation for walls and ceilings.

In the American presidential race and the Canadian election for Prime Minister in 1968, candidates took advantage of the paper dress "billboard" for their campaigns. Nixon and Trudeau saw ripping successes, but the gimmick didn't seem to work for Romney or Rockefeller.

Kaycel dresses by Mars of Asheville for George Romney's and Richard Nixon's campaigns for the Republican nomination, 1968
Reemay dress by James Sterling for Nelson Rockefeller's campaign for the Republican nomination, 1968
Reemay dress by James Sterling for Robert Kennedy's campaign for the Democratic nomination, 1968
Kaycel dress by Louben Industries, Montreal for Pierre Trudeau's campaign for the Liberal party, 1968

Paper mules and sandals designed by Kathryn Stoll for the New York shoe manufacturer Herbert Levine were tried out in the late summer of 1967.

Papier-mâché earrings and bracelet, late 1960s, unsigned

German paper dress, c. 1967

Although primarily an American fad, disposable garments were also being made in Mexico, Canada, England and Germany, usually of Reemay or other disposable materials due to shortages of paper Kaycel.

PAPER DUDS FOR DOGS

In 1967 a store in New York called 'Dogs of Distinction' carried in its stock, matching paper outfits for dog-and-mistress. The doggie outfits started at $2.95, the dresses at $6.95.

In 1967, Colorfashions produced boxed sets of jewellery aimed at the teen market. Designed by Gail E. Haley, the three-dimensional earrings, hair combs and necklaces were assembled from die-cut pieces punched out from high gloss printed card stock. At the higher end of the fashion scale was a popular trend for papier-mâché jewellery from designers such as Chrystya Olenska, Alma Davies, Doris Krupnick, and Betty Milham.

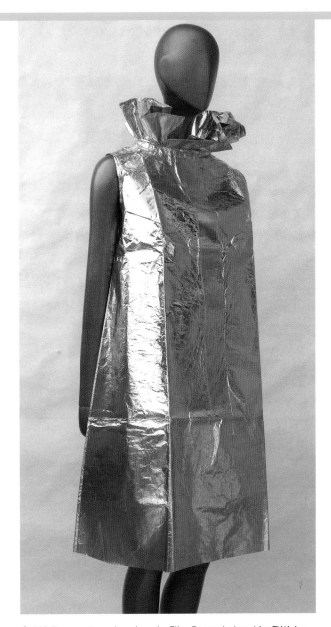

Kaycel paper sari designed by Elisa Daggs and made available for $5.00 from the Air India office in New York, 1967.

Gold foil paper stewardess dress by Elisa Daggs designed for TWA for first class service on transatlantic flights to Paris, 1967

BOAC and Trans World Airlines introduced paper uniforms for their stewardesses in 1967. The TWA stewardesses were even featured in their paper uniforms on the cover of a Boston Pops record album. Designed by Elisa Daggs, the TWA uniforms included a Greek key bordered white paper dress for Italian destinations, metallic gold tent dress with ruffled collar for French flights, a black jumpsuit with silver sash for New-York to Los Angeles Ambassador service, and a tropical flower print shift for Hawaiian furlongs. Elisa Daggs also designed a purple and lime green sari for Air India, not as a stewardess uniform but rather as a promotional campaign, available for $5.00 by mail order from the Air-India Public Relations department in New York.

Photographic print dresses, by Poster Dresses Ltd., London, England, 1967

Poster Dresses Ltd. was the first company to treat disposable dresses as large supergraphic canvasses. Their first release of fibron dresses in 1967 featured five photo prints including a rose, a cat, an eye, a rocket ship, and a hand in the Buddhist gesture of peace, with the super-imposed poem Uptown NY by "Beat" author Allen Ginsberg. Although a poster dress of Bob Dylan was also released separately from the series, another series of dresses as promised by Poster Dresses Ltd. never materialized.

END OF AN ERA

I n early 1968, the paper dress craze was beginning to cool. Many women who had tried the dresses found them less than satisfactory. An unidentified clipping from a magazine tucked in with a few unopened packages of paper dresses found at an estate sale told the story:

"Will nonsense become sense? There will be no turning back to a world of durable attire. Already washer manufacturers are worried over the prediction that by 1976 about 80 percent of all clothing will be paper...One of the girls at the office wore a paper shift. Before the evening was out a raggedy frizz developed just below the armpit of the garment. The thread of the seams held up better than the non-woven cellulose, which was plainly torn enough to expose a thigh too high. After three wearings, coffee stains, a cigarette burn, and general dishevelment unrepairable by even the recommended cool iron made the frock fit for the wastebasket, but it was almost as unseemly after the first wearing. So the girl threw it away, and for all that fun she blew $5.00... The real appeal (of paper fashion) is its arrogant obsolescence, combined with clever styling."

Although disposable garments were never intended for more than one wearing there seemed to be disappointment from buyers when this turned out to be true. The dresses billowed when the wearer sat and sleeved styles were uncomfortable. Paper suggested easy access, like gift-wrap on a parcel. Many women who wore a paper dress to

Dipsters bathing suits, c. 1978

a party recall unpleasant incidents of 'accidental' drink spills and tugs on hemlines to see how tear proof the material really was. Paper dresses could bring undue attention and the growing women's movement was supporting more sexually equalizing styles at the time.

As early as 1966 the Macy Bureau of Standards reported that paper clothes had inadequate fastness, and a 'crocking' tendency, which involved the exposure of the lining when the fabric is bent. The report was referred to by The New York Times on February 21, 1967 which cited from the report "Our approach to paper clothing is that it should be sold as a fun thing with no utility consideration and certainly not from the viewpoint of price advantage." Mildred Custin, president of Bonwit Teller was prophetically quoted in the same article "The demand has surprised us but I see it on a long term basis as more important in the industrial and utility field than in the fashion area... it will have a life for at least several seasons in specialized apparel categories but it may turn out to be just a fad".

Despite meteoric success as a promotional tool, the coupon offers in magazines for paper dresses dwindled and articles on the subject slowly disappeared throughout 1968. Two years after the start of the craze Joyce Carter, writer for Toronto's Globe Magazine wrote on May 4, 1968 "No one would seriously propose that disposable garments, at their present level of development should replace conventional clothing. What these do offer is wardrobe variety at mini-prices, sure to appeal to travelers and budget-bound fashion faddists." Carter never rallied to the trend but even she had to admit that there was a nugget of value in the experiment. The craze for paper clothing tore a strip out of the late 1960s and its foray into the fashion world was not a total loss. Paper dresses had stirred consumer excitement and the thought process of manufacturers and retailers to consider technological possibilities useful for modern living. The Canadian magazine Chatelaine reported in February 1968 "In the future, when our homes become dust-free and housework automated, white clothes will be practical – disposable or not. In future, materials that change colour to match surroundings, adjust to temperature changes, too, maybe available. Plastic may one day be extruded into flexible shapes for all types of clothes."

By 1969, the hippie movement with its back to nature viewpoint and strong anti-pollution message was effectively changing public perceptions on the

There was a successful business in souvenir jackets printed in the late 1980s and 1990s for special events using Tyvek®. The bonded plastic material was beneficial to those who arrived at an open air concert or sporting event without a raincoat.

Dipsters bathing suits, late 1970s

subject of a disposable society. The Disposables Association held a seminar in 1971 to address the shift in public opinion. One of the concerns was to change the name of the organization: "The word 'disposable' itself can be a red flag to the youth culture, because of the widespread concern with the problem of solid wastes". What had been associated with modernism was now seen as wasteful. However, as Scott and Kimberly-Stevens had publicly stated in 1966, a lasting business for disposable apparel remained in the industries for which it was originally developed in the late 1950s. The disposable clothing market did continue for industrial uses and it wasn't quite done with the fashion scene either.

In the Toronto magazine, Cityspan, a snippet appeared on August 12, 1978 that extolled the virtues of a bathing suit made of thin, opaque Tyvek® for hotel guests who didn't realize most hotels now had year-round swimming pools. 'Dipsters' brand bathing suits were available at $3.00 for men's trunks and $3.50 for women's bikinis. A pool

attendant at a Toronto Hotel claimed he sold sixty per month and that the suits moved well and were tough wearing. The writer of the article seemed to be completely oblivious of the disposable clothing fad just ten years earlier.

Painter's jumpsuits made of Tyvek® or Fibron made a fashion comeback in the early 1980s but mostly by fans of the New Wave music group Devo. Issey Miyake, who began using oiled paper in his collections as early as 1982 received a 1985 Fashion Design Council award for a white cocoon shaped Tyvek® dress. Other designers from Comme des Garcons to Norma Kamali experimented with paper in their collections during the 1980s but most of their sales went to museums rather than on the backs of the fashion-buying public.

1999 was the year of the non-woven revival. As we neared the year 2000 there was almost disappointment in the air that the future as envisioned by 1968's film '2001 A Space Odyssey'

What had been associated with modernism was now seen as wasteful.

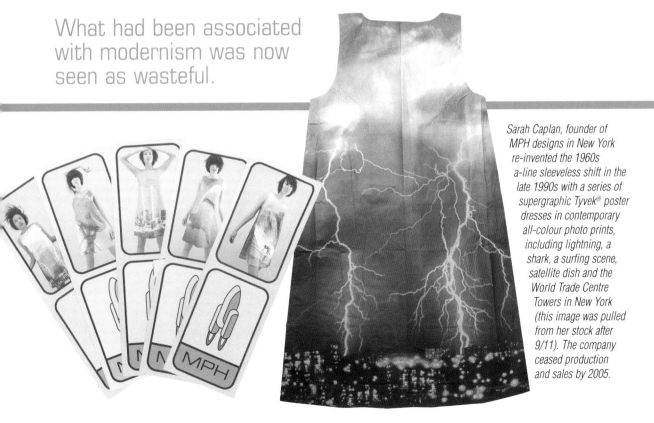

Sarah Caplan, founder of MPH designs in New York re-invented the 1960s a-line sleeveless shift in the late 1990s with a series of supergraphic Tyvek® poster dresses in contemporary all-colour photo prints, including lightning, a shark, a surfing scene, satellite dish and the World Trade Centre Towers in New York (this image was pulled from her stock after 9/11). The company ceased production and sales by 2005.

was nowhere to be seen. Perhaps subconsciously, designers using Tyvek® in their collections that year paid homage to 1960s futurism. Vivienne Tam used bright coloured floral printed Tyvek® in her 1999 collection that included an array of jackets, dresses, and separates ranging in price to upwards of $300.00. John Rocha and Krizia offered crinkled Tyvek® tops, playing up the papery qualities of the material and Hussein Chalayan created an affordable range of paper shift dresses and Velcro fastening trousers. Hugo Boss reinvented the man's paper suit for the Deutsche Guggenheim in Berlin which was featuring a retrospective exhibition of the pop-artist James Rosenquist in 1999. Rosenquist, who had been a pop art fixture in his paper suit during the late 1960s in New York, even helped to redesign the suit. Unfortunately, one buyer of the suit who wore it to the premiere of the Lion King in Toronto managed to rip out the seat of his pants in full view of the paparazzi lining the entrance to the theatre.

Amidst disappointing sales of non-woven yardage, Dupont sold its Reemay spunbonded technology in 1986. Eventually a British holding company acquired Reemay along with other non-woven manufacturers and created a division within the company called Fiberweb with the intent of creating a non-woven apparel market. Attempts since the 1990s have never taken off completely but the Holy Grail of a non-woven future still lurks on the horizon.

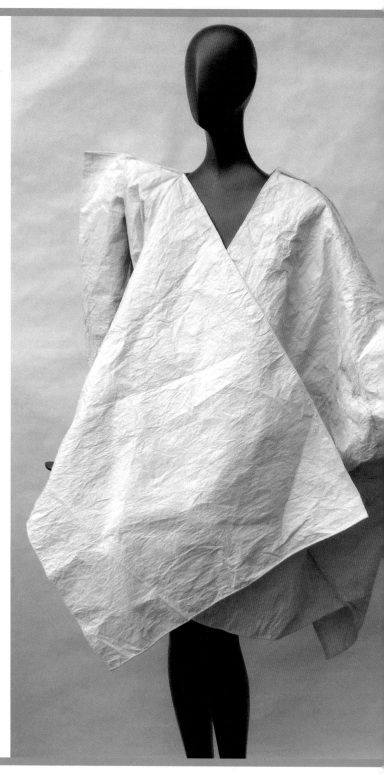

Tyvek paper coat by Issey Miyake, 1985

Acknowledgments

I am indebted for the tremendous hard work and vision of Phil Hacker for the layout of this book and Sue Barton for her patience in preparing the images for publication as well as Julia Pine for her work in editing and Kenn Norman for his help with proofing. I also want to thank Ivan Sayers who launched my interest in paper clothing when he gave me my first paper dress in April 1985. I would also like to thank the following for their help in the production of this book: Howell Conant who graciously allowed me to use the image on page twenty-four of the three models in their paper dresses which appeared in LIFE magazine; Whitehern Historic House & Garden, City of Hamilton, Ontario, for supplying the image of Anne Fletcher in her paper costume which appears on page five; The Brooklyn Museum, New York, for permission to use their image of the Andy Warhol painted dress in their collection which appears on page twenty-three; Susan Langley, Rochester, New York, who generously loaned the blue quilted paper dress on page eighteen for me to photograph for the book.

Bibliography

American Fabrics, Spring 1968 'Bonnie Cashin's Paper-Route to Fashion'

The Beautiful People, Marilyn Bender, Coward-McCann, NY, 1967

Chatelaine, February 1968, Vivian Wilcox

Cityspan, Toronto, August 12, 1978

Consumer Reports, 1966, www.consumerReports.org

Dress and Popular Culture, Bowling Green State University Popular Press 'Paper Clothes - Not Just a Fad' Alexandra Palmer, 1991

Du Pont of Canada, Chemistry and the Home, April 1967

Du Pont of Canada, Product Information Service Press release, August 6, 1969

The Evening Telegram, Toronto, May 6, 1936

The Everett Herald, Washington, June 28, 1966

The Everett Herald, Washington, May 24, 1967

The Everett Herald, Washington, June 9, 1967

The Financial Post, Toronto, 'She was only a Paper Doll', September 17, 1966

The Financial Post, Toronto, April 8, 1967

The Guardian, London, January 18, 2000

The Globe and Mail, 'Fashions to buy, wear, throw away gain favor', June 9, 1966, Zena Cherry

The Globe and Mail, 'Paper Clothing: fad or fashion?' February 21, 1967

The Globe and Mail, March 1968, Joyce Carter

The Globe Magazine, April 22, 1967, Joyce Carter

The Globe Magazine, May 4, 1968, Joyce Carter

Hair-Do Magazine, 'Be a Paper Doll', August 1967

Harper's Bazaar 'The Paper Shoe', July 1967

Harper's Bazaar 'September 1968'

J Walter Thompson Co. Ltd., Public Relations Department press release August 1, 1966

LIFE, 'Paper Jewelry and Chuck-Away Dresses', April 29, 1966

LIFE, 'The Wastebasket Dress Arrives' November 25, 1966, Helen Carlton

LOOK August 8, 1967

Newsday, Sept 25, 1999

'Not by Thread Alone' undated magazine clipping, c. 1968

The New York Times, September 6, 1966

The New York Times, January 22, 1967, 'Public Tries on Paper-Clothing Fad for Size' Isadore Barmash

The New York Times, February 21, 1967, Isadore Barmash

The New York Times, November 16, 1967 'Aboard the Michelangelo, Gowns Were Paper but Chic', Judy Klemestud

'Predictions from the past that haven't come true...yet', Sidney C. Schaer, future.newsday.com

Parade, 'Now you can live in a Paper House', June 18, 1967

Saturday Evening Post, December 2, 1967 'The Paper Caper', Anne Chamberlin

The Seattle Post Intelligencer, 'Futuristic Costume? Paper Dresses In' June 14, 1966

The Seattle Post Intelligencer, 'Paper Dollies Pay for Fun', May 25, 1967

The Seattle Post Intelligencer, May 30, 1967

The Seattle Post Intelligencer, Oct 15, 1967

TIME magazine, 'Real Live Paper Dolls' March 17, 1967

TW Special Report, The Innovators III, undated, c. 1969

West End Gazette, November 1915

About the Author

Jonathan Walford was born in 1961 in Vancouver, BC where he attended Simon Fraser University, receiving degrees in Canadian History and Museum Studies. He started working in the museum field in 1977 and has held curatorial positions with several institutions including the Bata Shoe Museum in Toronto. Mr. Walford is also a private collector of historic fashions from the 17th century to the present and has amassed a collection of over 6000 pieces ranging from the major couture houses of Paris to humble frocks from mail-order catalogues. He has lectured and published on the subject of historic costume and social history since 1980. He currently works as the Artistic Director of his company "Kickshaw Productions", which promotes the history of fashion through a variety of media and venues, and is currently founding the Fashion History Museum.

Other books by Jonathan Walford include: The Seductive Shoe – Four Centuries of Fashion Footwear, Thames and Hudson 2007. For more information: www.kickshawproductions.com